Higher
Education
for the
21st
Century

RAND

The Fiscal and Demographic Environment of the California State University at Northridge

*Stephen Carroll, Dominic Brewer,
Dana Soloff, Debra Strong*

Supported by the
California State University at Northridge
Lilly Endowment Inc.

Institute on Education and Training

Foreword

RAND's Institute on Education and Training (IET) conducts analytic research and provides technical assistance to improve education policy and practice in all sectors that offer education and training in the United States. Higher education is a major area of the IET's research. Over the next several years, the IET will publish a number of monographs on subjects ranging from new decisionmaking tools for higher education leaders to projections and analyses of demographic and fiscal trends. We will also report on large and small means for improving efficiency and effectiveness in postsecondary education. Finally, we will stimulate and participate in a needed debate over what the higher education system should be like in the next century—that is, why and how it should be redesigned.

These monographs will be published in the IET's *Higher Education for the 21st Century* series. This report, which is part of the series, presents the results of an examination of trends in fiscal and demographic factors that will affect the California State University at Northridge (CSUN). CSUN is engaged in a strategic planning process to develop coherent, coordinated responses to future challenges. The report is designed to provide information to those involved in the planning process. Specifically, we describe what the university's fiscal and enrollment patterns will be if no action is taken to modify current trends and policies. We do not suggest that the trends identified in this report are immutable. Rather, our purpose is to help planners decide whether the university's current policies and programs are consistent with the constellation of forces that will bear on its long-term future.

The study is designed to help CSUN planners assess the long-term implications of current demographic and fiscal trends. The report should be of interest to policymakers concerned about higher education's overall long-term fiscal future.

iv

The work reported here was jointly supported by the California State University at Northridge and RAND's Institute on Education and Training with funds from a grant by the Lilly Endowment, Inc.

Roger Benjamin
Director, Institute on Education and Training

Stephen Carroll
Senior Economist

Contents

Figures

Tables

Summary

Strategic planning provides a framework for institutions, including institutions of higher education, to shape their futures in a coordinated, comprehensive, and consistent manner. Effective planning cannot be simply imposed from the top: It must involve all stakeholders at all stages of the process. It is essential that all those involved operate from a common set of assumptions about the complex of factors that affect an institution's future. Among the most critical are external environmental factors. For institutions of higher education, especially public institutions, these may include fiscal, demographic, labor market, political, legal, technological, and social forces, among others.

This report presents the results of an examination of some of these external forces that we conducted for the Northridge campus of the California State University. Resource constraints dictated that we focus on three of the many possible forces likely to affect the institution's future: fiscal and demographic trends, and the political context.[1] Our purpose was to describe the existing state of affairs for each of the three and to try to project recent trends into the future. It is important to note that the intent and results of this analysis are purely descriptive: It is designed to provide a common base of information about the environment for planners—not to offer specific suggestions about how the institution should respond to trends that the analysis identifies.

Results of the Analysis

The results of this analysis paint a challenging picture for the state and its institutions of higher education, including the California State University at Northridge (CSUN).

Fiscal Trends

For the state, fiscal trends suggest a looming financial crisis:

- Major spending programs will grow faster than state revenues.

---

[1]We also prepared a brief memorandum discussing labor market trends in CSUN's "catchment area."

- Mandated expenditures and entitlements will consume almost all General Fund revenues (which represent virtually all of the budget over which the governor and legislature have any control).

- The results of these and other trends will be a growing squeeze on public services, particularly higher education.

Under these circumstances, our projections show that the share of the budget allocated to higher education will be cut *at least* in half over the next decade. For the California State University (CSU) as a whole, our optimistic estimate is that its share of General Fund revenues will drop in inflation-adjusted dollars from $1.4 billion in 1995 to just over $1 billion by 2005. Our pessimistic forecast is that it will drop to $600 million. If CSUN's *percentage* of the CSU funding remains constant, its General Fund revenues could drop from a high of $170 million in 1989 to $130 million by 2005, in our optimistic scenario, or to $100 million, in our pessimistic scenario.

Demographic Trends

Many demographic factors could conceivably affect undergraduate enrollment demand at CSUN, including distribution of the population in terms of age, income, occupation, race, and ethnicity. CSUN draws 72 percent (1993) of its first-time freshmen from Los Angeles/Ventura–area high schools and a consistent 73 percent of its transfer students from community and four-year colleges in roughly the same area. Thus, local demographics will affect its enrollments and the age and ethnic mix of its student population. Our projections identify two major demographic trends that can be expected to affect enrollment directly:

- The population age group that has traditionally composed the bulk of CSUN's total enrollment is shrinking and will continue to shrink over the foreseeable future.

- The ethnic composition of this population is changing dramatically. Hispanics will comprise an increasingly large proportion of the population into the next century. Because Hispanic enrollment rates in CSUN have historically been lower than rates of other ethnic groups, this increase seems unlikely to create a corresponding increase in total enrollments.

Given the fact that almost three-quarters of CSUN students come from the local area, the local employment opportunities for college graduates might affect enrollment and program demand. However, the link between local labor-market opportunities and demand for enrollment in local institutions has not been empirically established. Further, we had no way of tracking where CSUN alumni have taken jobs in the past. At the request of CSUN, we did provide a brief analysis of the local labor market, but those results are not part of this analysis.

Political Context

We have presented the information summarized above to various legislators and other policymakers throughout the state. Their response has not been very sanguine about the state's fiscal future or the challenges facing the state's higher-education system. There are many constraints on political response:

- Demographics imply increased demand for health and welfare services and K–12 education. Cuts in benefits for the former have been offset by that increase, and per-pupil spending levels for K–12 education are mandated (by state Propositions 98 and 111).

- California cannot expect much help from the federal government. Block grants might increase health and welfare program flexibility but will most likely mean further cuts in actual resources. Some federal budget actions (e.g., proposed changes in Medicare) could actually make the state's financial situation worse.

- Policymakers realize that the "three strikes" sentencing legislation requires corrections spending that will be consuming 21 percent of the state's annual budget by 2005. However, the public is not in the mood to see that law revised.

Under the circumstances, higher education's piece of the public pie will shrink and the CSU system is likely to be hardest hit, for two reasons: (1) The community colleges share the protection of Proposition 98. (2) Many policymakers see the University of California (UC) system as the "crown jewel" of the state's higher education enterprise, and it is having severe problems of its own. CSU's needs may well take second place to UC's.

State officials, elected office holders, and educational policymakers with whom we have met do understand that the CSU system is highly vulnerable in this environment. However, neither legislators nor educational administrators or policy makers at the state lavel have yet focused their attention on a systematic analysis of the problems confronting CSU.

Implications

Our projections suggest that CSUN, along with the rest of the state's higher-education system, faces an unsettling fiscal future. Besides fiscal constraints, CSUN must also contend with *decreasing* demand for enrollment. Because the CSU system as a whole faces *increased* demand, which greatly outruns its capacity to provide facilities and services, CSUN may find its relative share of resources reduced through reallocation to other campuses.

Most of our findings point to one clear implication: CSUN cannot expect to continue "business as usual." The state's fiscal problems are likely to get worse and total support from the state will decline in real terms—perhaps substantially. Nothing in the foreseeable future offers hope of a fiscal turnaround or state action that will substantially change the scenario. In this context, pressures will be high for all the state's higher-education institutions to do more with less.

While the environmental picture is clear, the implications for CSUN's strategic planning must be defined by those involved in the planning process. The environmental analysis is intended to help them by establishing common assumptions to guide their deliberations.

Acknowledgments

We have received assistance and advice from numerous CSUN faculty, staff, and administrators. President Blenda Wilson; Provost Louanne Kennedy; Pat Nichelson, Chair of the Strategic Planning Committee; and the members of that committee provided both guidance and feedback to us throughout the analysis. We are particularly grateful to Hans Ladanyi, Director of Institutional Research at CSUN, and to his staff, for providing much of the data we used in the study and helping us understand the strengths and weaknesses of various data sources.

Several RAND colleagues contributed to the development and implementation of this analysis. We are particularly indebted to Maryann Jacobi Gray and Larry Hanser for their valuable comments on an earlier draft of this report, to Joyce Peterson for overseeing the organization and final preparation of this report, to Sandra Cutuli for her editorial assistance, and to Tracy Jenkins, who prepared the figures and tables as well as the final text.

The work reported here was led by Roger Benjamin, director of RAND's Institute on Education and Training. We are particularly indebted to him for his intellectual leadership throughout the course of the effort.

While we recognize the contributions of the many people who made this report possible, we emphasize that the discussion and findings in this report reflect only the views of the authors.

1. Introduction

Motivation and Context for Strategic Planning

California State University at Northridge is one of 21 campuses in the California State University system. Founded on July 1, 1958, the 353-acre campus is located in the community of Northridge, an unincorporated area in the San Fernando Valley with a population of some 82,000 (1995 projection). Eight schools and 49 departments make up the academic structure of the university, which has 894 full-time-equivalent faculty members, or FTE, and an annual budget of $151 million (FY 1995). In the fall of 1995, the university enrolled a total of 20,019 undergraduates (15,565 FTE) and 4,996 graduate students (2,482 FTE).

CSUN's president of 23 years retired in 1992. A new president took the helm as the university struggled to adapt to changing fiscal and demographic conditions. For most of its history, CSUN had seen steady enrollment increases.[1] In 1985, CSUN's FTE enrollment stood at 20,402.[2] But by 1990, enrollment began a decline from which the university has not emerged.

In addition, CSUN saw the demographics of its student population change (for instance, its population of minority and immigrant students increased), and along with the entire CSU system, the university faced tighter budgets and tuition increases. Changing enrollment patterns included shifting demands among academic programs.

In 1993, the president initiated a strategic planning process that was to involve all university departments and stakeholders. But before the new president's planning effort could get under way, the university was literally shaken to its core by the massive Northridge earthquake of January 17, 1994. Quake damage on campus was estimated at $350 million. Dramatic photos of a collapsed parking structure on the campus flashed across the nation. In all, several buildings were either destroyed or damaged so extensively that the university would be unable to use them without substantial reconstruction and repair.

---

[1]Though a strategic planning effort had been undertaken in the 1970s as a response to short-term declines in enrollment growth.

[2]*California Almanac*, 1985 edition, page 75.

In various ways, the need to physically rebuild the campus underlined how crucial strategic planning is to an institution's long-term well-being. Grim though the earthquake was, it provided an opportunity—and a challenge—to reconfigure CSUN to meet its future, rather than to reconstruct the past.

Some eight months after the quake, the strategic planning effort got under way. CSUN's leadership asked RAND to join with two consulting firms in a joint effort to support the university's strategic planning process.

RAND's primary role was to offer technical support by providing a comprehensive and objective base of internal and external information from which planning participants could draw. This role involved various research and evaluation tasks, including the identification and description of the planning environment, and the provision of information on trends, issues, opportunities, and constraints facing CSUN. The research focused particularly on student demographics and the fiscal environment at the institutional, system-wide, and state levels. The two consulting firms were asked by CSUN to provide facilitation and management of the on-campus planning process.

The purpose of this report is to present the results of an environmental analysis that provides a critical basis for the CSUN strategic planning process. This introduction describes our concept of strategic planning and the function of the external analysis, how it fits into the higher-education planning context, and the elements of the analysis that we performed for CSUN.

Strategic Planning and the Role of the External Analysis

Strategic planning provides a framework for institutions to deal with the many challenges they face in a coordinated and consistent way. Our approach to strategic planning emphasizes that it cannot be imposed from the top. It necessarily involves participation of all stakeholders at all stages of the process—in the university's case, this includes faculty, students, administrative units, and the community. Further, strategic planning is a multi-layered process with many supporting tasks, primarily the following:

- clarifying the institution's mission and vision of its future;
- identifying the internal strengths and weaknesses of the institution and the barriers to change;
- mapping the institution's external environment and how that is likely to change; and
- developing a comparative information system that enables priority-setting.

In this report, we are concerned with the third task: In order for any institution to make informed planning decisions about its future, it needs a systematic understanding of the environment it faces and how that environment is likely to change in the future. Of course, planners have some control over certain aspects of their environment. Many forces, however, are external to the institution itself—factors that have a powerful effect on how an institution develops but that cannot be controlled directly by decisionmakers within the institution. An examination of these forces forms the basis of our analysis of the external environment.

The analysis represents a single but critical component of the strategic planning process: It is designed to provide a common base of information for planners. Put another way, the analysis is intended to present plausible scenarios about future trends in the factors that will affect CSUN's future. It is not intended to provide an exhaustive account of all the factors affecting the institution's environment, nor to offer specific suggestions as to how CSUN should behave or respond to trends the analysis identifies. In other words, the intent of this analysis is not prescriptive in any way.

The CSUN Environmental Analysis

Complete characterization of an institution's external environment would require examining an extremely broad array of forces, e.g., economic/financial, demographic, political, technological, legal, social, and cultural forces at many levels—local, state, national, and even international.

Initial discussions with planners at CSUN led us to focus on two *major* domains for the environmental analysis:

- California's fiscal future and its projected effect on CSUN's financial resources; and

- demographic projections and their effect on enrollment demand at CSUN.

The fiscal context clearly affects an institution's ability to provide quality undergraduate and graduate education. Available funds affect the opportunities to develop new programs, upgrade existing facilities and programs, hire and reward qualified faculty, and so on. Demographic changes, in terms of both the potential number of students and their composition, directly affect admissions policies, curriculum offerings, strategies to deal with diversity, student support services and retention policies, etc.

4

The analysis describes the current fiscal and demographic environment and attempts to outline the future environment if current trends do not change dramatically. Besides demographic and fiscal changes, the analysis includes a brief discussion of California's political context.

Section 2 presents the results of our analysis for fiscal and demographic trends, with some discussion of political factors as well. The final section discusses the implications of these results for CSUN's planning efforts.

2. CSUN's Future Environment

In developing a strategic plan, CSUN's planners must take account of fiscal, demographic, and political trends that will affect the institution. In this section, we discuss California's general fiscal future and how it is likely to affect support of higher education in general and CSUN in particular, and the demographic trends likely to affect CSUN's enrollment. We also comment briefly on the political context that may affect possible state policy responses.

California's Fiscal Picture

As one campus of the state university system, CSUN relies largely on public dollars for its main source of revenue. We therefore begin by discussing the general health of the state's economy and budgetary picture, drawing implications for higher education in general, the CSU system as a whole, and CSUN in particular.

Our analysis indicates that three major long-term trends will significantly shape California's fiscal environment and hence the environment of the state's higher-education systems. First, state General Fund revenues will grow slowly to moderately, at best. Second, receiver populations (those who are net consumers of state health, social, and welfare support services) will grow at least as fast as will General Fund revenues. Third, corrections costs will grow rapidly. These trends will have the following effects:

- faster growth in demand for state services than in revenues to support those services;
- disproportionate growth in mandated and entitlement spending; and
- a growing financial squeeze on public services.

The result will be reduced funding available for California's public higher-education system. Moreover, the fiscal constraints will have a proportionately greater effect on the California State University (CSU) system than on the University of California (UC) or the community colleges. Understanding the dynamics of these fiscal changes requires some background on education funding in the state.

Historical Background

When California's Master Plan for Higher Education was drafted in 1960, the role of state and local government in California and across the nation was set to expand dramatically. California's population growth and economic expansion, coupled with inflation and increasing property values, led to continued increases in the state's tax base, providing increased revenues to support higher education and other state programs and services. But during the 1970s, a series of events combined to change the fiscal structure and scenario in California.

In June 1978, eyeing a state budget surplus of several billion dollars and confronted with dramatic escalation in property tax liabilities, the state's voters passed Proposition 13. Proposition 13 rolled back assessed property values to 1975–1976 levels, limited the rate of property taxation to 1 percent, and capped increases in assessed valuation at no more than 2 percent annually. Proposition 13 also limited the ability of state and local government to levy taxes on local property and imposed super-majority requirements to approve many types of tax increases.

As a result, property tax revenues fell in 1978 by about 57 percent. A complex new system of property taxation and state support was put into place. Each county collected the local property taxes allowed under Proposition 13 and distributed the proceeds among local governments and special districts in proportion to their respective shares of the county's property tax revenues the prior year. The state set funding targets for local entities and provided support from state revenues and surpluses to make up the difference between a local entity's target and its post–Proposition 13 tax revenues. The targets established for most types of local governments were generally based on estimates of the property tax revenues that an agency would have received had Proposition 13 not been enacted. In some cases, the targets were set to accomplish additional state objectives. For example, local school district revenue targets were determined in accordance with *Serrano* and subsequent court decisions.[3]

Constrained by Proposition 13, other tax and expenditure limitations, and a political climate increasingly hostile to tax increases, state and local governments had little room to increase tax revenues, even in line with inflation. By the late 1980s, the state's ability to subsidize schools and local governments was in

---

[3]In *Serrano v. Priest*, filed in 1968, decided in 1971, and re-affirmed on appeal in 1976, the California Supreme Court declared that the state's school finance system was unconstitutional. Because local schools were financed by local property revenues, the court ruled that the quality of a student's education was dependent on the property wealth of the city in which he or she lived. Thus, school spending was to be equalized through a system of state, rather than local, finance.

jeopardy. In order to protect education's share of tax revenues, in 1988 school supporters qualified and voters passed Proposition 98 and, subsequently, Proposition 111, which set a floor for K–14 education spending.

The tax limitation movement and poor economic conditions combined to severely limit tax revenues of all sorts for the state to fund its programs and services. In 1992, the state responded to its own budget crisis by essentially running the post–Proposition 13 bailout in reverse.[4] It shifted $1.3 billion in property tax revenues from local governments to K–12 schools and community colleges, allowing the state to reduce its own contribution to schools but still meet the Proposition 98 requirements.

California's Budget: The Distribution of the General Fund

California's receipts and expenditures can be grouped into four categories (as they are in the governor's budget):

- *Federal funds* are all funds received directly from an agency of the federal government. These funds are passed through the state budget (usually to local governments) for schools, the federal share of payments for Aid to Families with Dependent Children (AFDC), and so forth.

- *Bond funds* are used to finance projects, such as prison construction or park land acquisition, for which the bonds were authorized.

- *Special-fund* revenues are restricted by state law for particular functions or activities of government. Motor vehicle–related levies are the primary source of special-fund revenues.

- *The General Fund* comprises the remaining funds included in California's annual budget. The General Fund contains the funds open to state control, and the budget that the Governor presents and the legislature adopts each year consists of its General Fund revenues and expenditures.

For purposes of our analysis, we have divided General Fund expenditures into five categories:

The **health and welfare** category includes the range of state-supported health and welfare programs mandated by federal law. For example, the state Medi-Cal program, Supplemental Security Income (SSI), and California's share of AFDC are included in this category.

---

[4] Arthur O'Sullivan, "The Future of Proposition 13 in California" (*The California Policy Seminar CPS Brief*, Vol. 5, No. 4, March 1993).

8

The **corrections** category includes operating expenditures for incarcerating convicted felons and supervising them on parole after their release from prison. It also includes the Youth Authority and youth corrections system.

The **higher education** category includes state support of UC and CSU and several other institutions such as the state library, the California Maritime Academy, and the California Postsecondary Education Commission.

Because Proposition 98 covers funding for community colleges, as well as K–12 education, we include the community colleges in the category **K–14 education** rather than in higher education.

All other spending, including interest on state debt and the costs of operating state government, fall in the **other** category.

Figure 1 shows each category's 1995 share of General Fund expenditures. Table 1 indicates how General Fund allocations shifted among the five categories, from 1970 to 1981 (two years after the passage of Proposition 13) to 1995.[5]

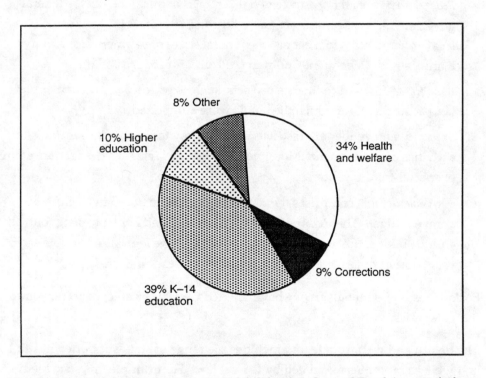

Figure 1—Projected FY 95 Distribution of California's General Fund Appropriations

Source: Department of Finance, State of California, *Governor's Budget: 1995-96*, Sacramento, California, 1995.

---

[5]Because it took two years for the state to fully work out its response to Proposition 13, we show the distribution of General Fund allocations in FY 1981.

Table 1

Changes in General Fund Expenditure Shares, 1970–1995

Budget Category	Share of General Fund (%)		
	FY 70	FY 81	FY 95
Health and Welfare	30	33	34
Corrections	4	3	9
K–14 education	37	40	39
Higher education	14	10	10
Other	15	13	8

Source: Department of Finance, State of California, *Governor's Budget*, Sacramento, California, annual.

General Fund Revenues and Expenditures

In making the revenue and expenditure projections in this report, we assume that current demographic and economic trends, tax policies, and mandated spending programs all continue through the next decade. Thus, we project the implications of these assumptions through 2005.

From 1995 and beyond, we project a modest increase in General Fund revenues.[6] These revenue projections are in line with those of several similar econometric forecasts for California.

Figure 2 depicts these General Fund increases to 2005. Although the history of business cycles in the postwar decades suggests that an economic slowdown is likely during this period, we did not attempt to project the timing or magnitude of either recessions or expansions. Therefore, even though the General Fund revenue projections were estimated conservatively, they are in some sense optimistic because economic conditions will fluctuate more than the figure's trend line suggests.

---

[6]We estimated future General Fund revenues in three steps. First, we modeled the effects of economic and demographic factors on personal income per capita in California. We then entered alternative projections of economic trends and the State Department of Finance's demographic projections to estimate future per capita personal income. Third, we used a series of models to estimate the revenues that would be raised by each of the state's taxes, given estimates of per capita personal incomes. The data and procedures we used to estimate future General Fund revenues are detailed in Stephen Carroll et al., *Projecting California's Fiscal Future*, MR-570-LE, RAND, 1995.

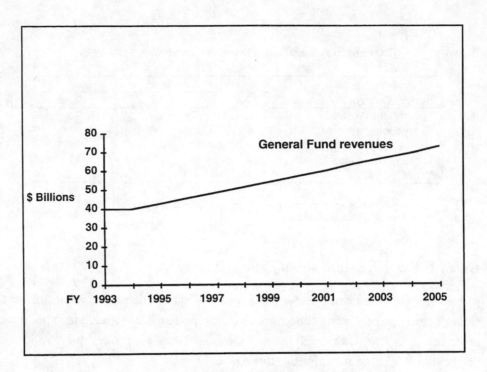

Figure 2—Anticipated Revenue Increase
(smoothed trend)

How will this rise in revenues compare with anticipated growth in state spending for health and welfare, corrections, and K–14 education? Figures 3, 4, and 5 present our projections.[7] Because the magnitude of spending in each category differs, we base the comparison on an index, rather than absolute amounts, to compare spending increases in these categories with increases in General Fund revenues. For all categories, 1994 serves as the base year. Thus, an index value of, say, 140 for spending on health and welfare indicates that, in a given year, health and welfare expenditures represent 140 percent of 1994 expenditures.

---

[7]See Stephen Carroll et al.,1995 for a detailed discussion of the data and procedures used to estimate future General Fund spending in each of these categories.

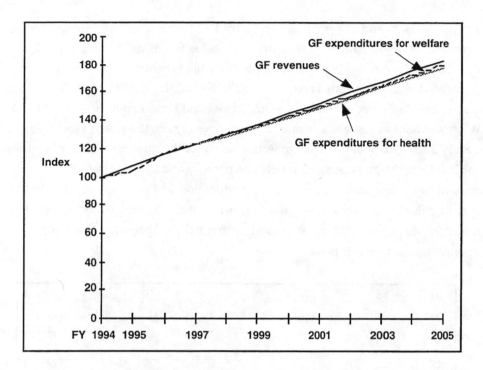

Figure 3—Comparison of Anticipated Increases in General Fund Revenues and General Fund Expenditures for Health and Welfare

Health and welfare expenditures are likely to increase at about the same rate as General Fund revenues.[8] As a matter of fact, Figure 3 graphically illustrates that the rates of increase can hardly be distinguished from one another. Although our projection assumes cuts in benefits consistent with cuts in AFDC benefits since 1987, and cuts in SSI (Supplemental Security Income) provided by federal funds, and SSP (State Supplemental Program) which supplements SSI and comes from the General Fund since 1989, the growth in receiver populations has more than offset these benefit reductions. Currently, General Fund support makes up around 55 percent of CSU funding. Tuition and student fees provide about 15%, and self-financing revenues (from dormitories, book stores and food service, for instance) provide another 25 percent. These self-financing revenues may not be used for instructional purposes. Finally, "other" state revenues and federal funds make up the remaining 4 and 1 percent, respectively.

---

[8]We applied past trends in participation rates in each of the state's major health and welfare programs to the State Department of Finance's demographic projections to estimate the numbers of participants in each program in each future year. We extrapolated past trends in the benefits each participant received to estimate future benefits payments. We multiplied these estimates to project total future expenditures in each program. Finally, we added the estimates across programs to project total future health and total future welfare expenditures.

12

Propositions 98 and 111 establish a base for K–14 education and guarantee that spending on K–14 education will grow at least as fast as inflation and K–12 enrollments. To the extent that local property tax revenues fall short of mandated levels, the state is required to fill the funding gap from General Fund revenues. As Figure 4 indicates, required General Fund expenditures for K–14 will rise about as fast as General Fund revenues (again, the rates of increase are barely distinguishable).[9] This projection assumes the minimum level of support for K–14 education prescribed by Propositions 98 and 111. Under this assumption, per-pupil funding for K–12 education will grow no faster than the rate of inflation. However, because California currently ranks 42nd among the states in per pupil spending, it is possible that political pressure to increase K–12 spending could raise this rate.

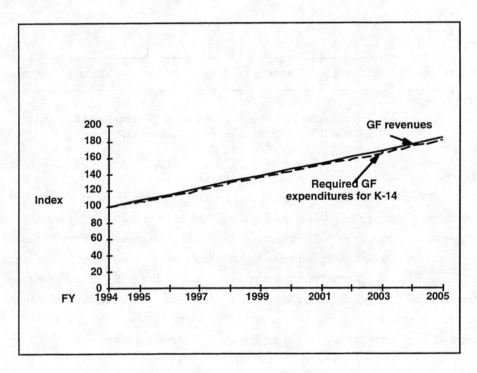

Figure 4—Required K–4 Expenditures Will Rise as Fast as General Fund Revenues

The share of the budget spent on corrections began to grow rapidly in the early 1980s, when determinant sentencing was introduced. In March 1994, the California legislature mandated lengthy sentences for repeat felons. Put forward

---

[9]We built a model of required Proposition 98/111 spending for K–14 education and used our estimates of future per-capita personal incomes and the Legislative Analyst's Office's estimates of future K–12 enrollments to project future K–14 spending requirements. We then estimated future property tax revenues available for K–14 and subtracted these estimates from the projected spending requirements to obtain estimates of the required state spending for K–14.

with the slogan "three strikes and you're out," the legislation prescribed that felons found guilty of a third serious crime be locked up for 25 years to life. In November 1994, the state's voters enacted a ballot proposition that strongly endorsed such stiff sentencing measures and wrote the requirements into the state's constitution. A RAND study has estimated that this law will roughly double the fraction of the state General Fund consumed by the Department of Corrections.[10] It will increase not only the number of felons incarcerated but also—even more significantly—the length of sentences served. Figure 5 illustrates how drastically California's "three-strikes" initiative will affect state corrections spending. It shows that, in marked contrast to the other categories considered thus far, corrections spending will increase at a substantially higher rate than the General Fund.

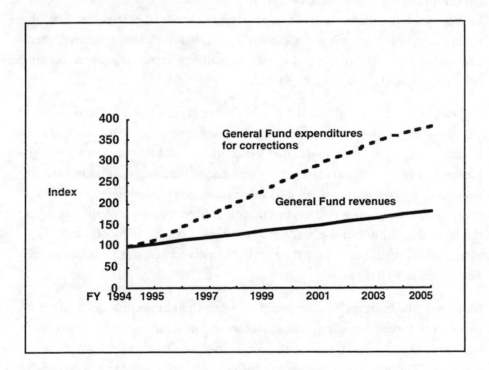

Figure 5—Spending on Corrections Will Grow Much Faster Than Revenues

Table 2 shows the projected shares of General Fund revenues for the five budget categories in FY 2005 and their respective shares in 1995. As the table suggests, in 2005 the share of General Fund revenues left over for higher education and "other" after expenditures on health and welfare, corrections, and K–14 education, will be no more than 9 percent.

---

[10]Peter W. Greenwood et al., *Three Strikes and You're Out: Estimated Benefits and Costs of California's New Mandatory-Sentencing Law*, MR-509-RC, RAND, 1994.

Table 2

**General Fund Budget Shares by Category;
Actual for 1995; Projected 2005**

	Share of General Fund %	
Budget Category	FY 95	FY 05
Health and Welfare	34	32
Corrections	9	20
K–14 education	39	39
Higher education	10	?
Other	8	?

All in all, these trends add up to a looming budget crisis for California. Major spending programs will grow faster than state revenues. Mandated expenditures and entitlements will consume almost all General Fund revenues, as receiver populations continue to grow and as the sentencing effects of "three strikes" are felt. Proposition 98 leaves California little flexibility with regard to K–14 education. The result of these trends will be a growing squeeze on public services, particularly on higher education.

It should be emphasized that the breakdown of specific assumptions underlying the foregoing analysis does little to alter the scenario. For instance, legal and political observers may suggest that the courts will not fully enforce the "three strikes initiative," so that increases in corrections funding will be lower than projected. Under such conditions, higher education spending may not be "squeezed" to the same degree, but it is difficult to argue, given the magnitude of the spending shifts and shortfalls, that changes in one or a few of these assumptions would eliminate the shortfalls or even necessarily reduce them to any meaningful degree.

Moreover, the budget situation could be worse than projected. As mentioned earlier, our forecast assumes that any economic downturns will be balanced by economic expansions. California's budget may also be affected by natural disasters. Budget projections for the current fiscal year assume a level of federal support for immigration costs that is unlikely to be forthcoming. Several major court challenges have the potential to cost California several billion dollars.[11] Governor Wilson has also proposed a 15 percent tax cut, which would have little immediate effect on the budget but could have a much greater effect on revenues over the following five years. Finally, efforts at the federal level to replace social funding with block grants and to balance the federal budget by reducing spending may substantially reduce revenues flowing to California from the

---

[11]Kathleen Connell (California State Controller), "1995–96 State Budget: Enormous Risks Loom," *Controller's Quarterly*, April 1995, pp. 4–5.

federal government. As stark as they seem, our projections may actually paint an optimistic future, given these potential shocks.

CSU's Funding Future

As Figure 6 shows, the two primary sources of funding for the CSU system are state General Fund revenues, which represented about 70 percent of funding until 1981, and student fees and tuition, representing about 5 percent until 1981.[12] Currently, General Fund support makes up around 55 percent of CSU funding, tuition and student fees provide about 15 percent, and self-financing revenues (from dormitories, book stores and food service, for instance) provide another 25 percent. These self-financing revenues may not be used for instructional purposes. Finally, "other" state revenues and federal funds make up the remaining 4 and 1 percent, respectively. Thus, CSU's fiscal future is clearly related to, and dependent upon, California's overall fiscal health.

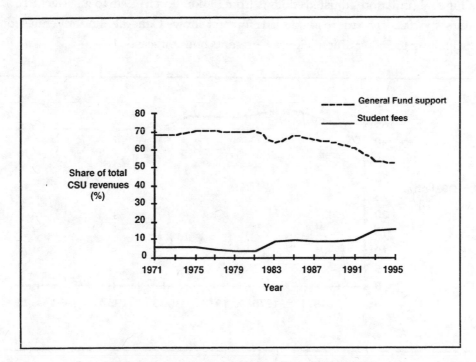

Figure 6—Sources of CSU Funding, 1971 to 1995

Source: California Postsecondary Education Commission, *Fiscal Profiles: 1994*, Report 94-17, Sacramento, CA, October 1994.

---

[12]Division of Analytic Studies, Office of the Chancellor, California State University, *Statistical Reports: 1994–95*, Long Beach, Calif., 1995.

16

In terms of the level of financial support the CSU system can expect from state general revenues, the picture is grim. By fiscal year 2005, projections based on current trends indicate that the share of General Fund revenues available for higher education/other categories combined will be around 9 percent.

We consider two scenarios about higher education's share of that 9 percent: Under an optimistic scenario, higher education's share declines to 5 percent, half its current share, over the next decade. This leaves only 4 percent in 2005 for other demands on the General Fund. Under a pessimistic scenario, we assume that "other" is allocated 6 percent in 2005, leaving only 3 percent for higher education.

What share of this shrinking pie supports the CSU system? Since 1967, CSU's share of total higher education funding has ranged between 45 and 50 percent (Figure 7). Assuming that CSU continues to receive its traditional share of higher education funding, the optimistic forecast is that its General Fund revenues will fall in real (inflation-adjusted) dollars from $1.4 billion in 1995 to just over $1 billion by 2005. The more pessimistic forecast shows General Fund revenues for CSU falling to $600 million. Figure 8 presents both forecasts.

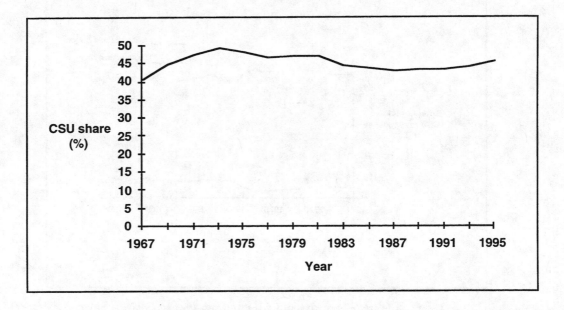

Figure 7—CSU Share of General Fund Expenditures on Higher Education

Source: California Postsecondary Education Commission, *Fiscal Profiles: 1994*, Report 94-17, Sacramento, Calif., October 1994.

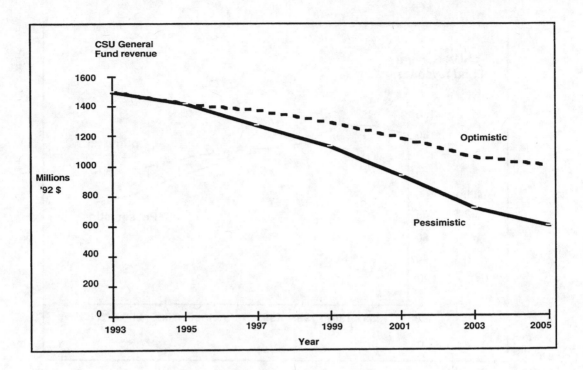

Figure 8—CSU's General Fund Revenues Will Fall Sharply

The Northridge Scenario

What about the direct effect on CSUN? Its share of CSU funding has remained level at just under 7.5 percent since 1987.[13] In the optimistic scenario, with no increase or decrease in the share of CSU funding that CSUN receives, relative to the funding given to its sister campuses, we can expect CSUN's General Fund revenues to drop from a high of over $170 million in 1989 to $130 million by 2005 (see Figure 9). In the pessimistic scenario, CSUN General Fund revenues could fall to around $100 million by 2005. The bottom line: significant decline in real revenues available to this campus over the next ten years, if current trends continue.

---

[13]Division of Analytic Studies, Office of the Chancellor, California State University, *Statistical Reports: 1994–95*, Long Beach, CA, 1995.

18

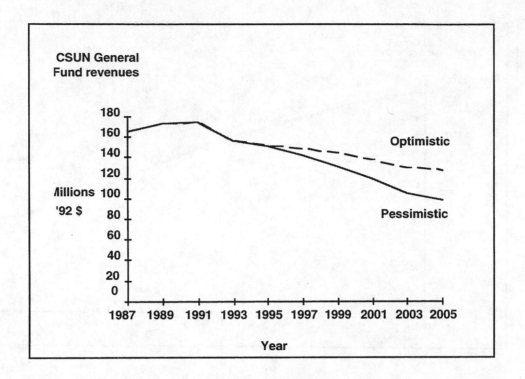

Figure 9—CSUN's Total General Fund Revenues Likely to Drop

Local Demographics and Enrollment Demand at CSUN

Many demographic factors could conceivably affect undergraduate enrollment demand at CSUN, including distribution of the population in terms of age, income, occupation, race, and ethnicity. Two major demographic trends can be expected to affect enrollment demand directly: (1) The population age group that has traditionally made up the bulk of CSUN's total enrollment is shrinking and will continue to shrink over the foreseeable future. (2) The ethnic composition of this population is changing dramatically. Both trends have important planning implications for CSUN.[14]

---

[14]The projections in this report are intended only to isolate and illustrate the potential effects of demographic changes in CSUN's prime catchment areas on future demand for CSUN services. They are not intended to project actual future enrollments. In order to focus on the demographic impact, other factors that might affect CSUN enrollment rates were assumed to be constant. These factors include tuition rates, the availability of financial aid, trends in family incomes, and so forth. For information regarding the potential effects of other factors in the near term, readers are referred to CSUN's Office of Institutional Research, *Enrollment Projections for 1995-96 to 1998-99* (April 10, 1995).

The Age Mix

In terms of age, CSUN's current undergraduate population is concentrated in the 18-to-29 age range, with enrollments coming primarily from those 20 to 24 years old. Figure 10 illustrates the age distribution of CSUN's undergraduates in odd years from 1987 to 1993.

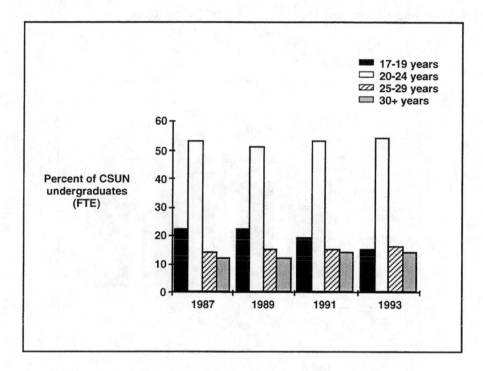

Figure 10—Age Profile of CSUN Undergraduate Enrollees, 1987–1993

Source: CSUN Office of Institutional Research

Like any "business," CSUN has a primary market area from which it draws the bulk of its enrollment. Based on historical trends, the "catchment area" consists of the San Fernando Valley and East Ventura County, with some "fingers" extending out into Santa Monica and metropolitan Los Angeles. Over the past decade, the sources of CSUN enrollment within this catchment area have been stable: 77 (1984) to 72 (1993) percent of first-time freshmen have come from 90 Los Angeles/Ventura–area high schools, and a consistent 73 percent of transfer students have come from 34 Los Angeles/Ventura–area community and four-year colleges.

The population in this area closely follows overall trends in Los Angeles County, and much of the data for this section is drawn from county data.

One identified trend is the decline in population among CSUN's primary enrollment group, those 20 to 24 years old. This population showed a clear upward trend from 1970, peaked in 1990, and is predicted to drop off sharply by 2000, recovering somewhat by 2005 (see Figure 11). The "echo" of the "baby boom" will hit Los Angeles County later than the rest of the state (by 2005 and beyond), for reasons that are unclear but may have to do with patterns of residence and family formation during the 1970s and 1980s.

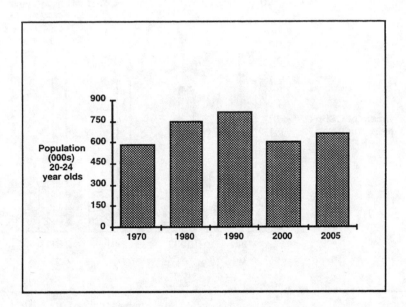

Figure 11—Changing Population of Those 20-24 Years Old in Los Angeles County

Source: California Department of Finance, Demographic Research Unit, *Population Projection*, March 1995.

More generally, the population of those 18 to 29 years old will drop sharply by 2000, then rebound and flatten out in both Los Angeles and Ventura Counties, as shown in Figure 12.

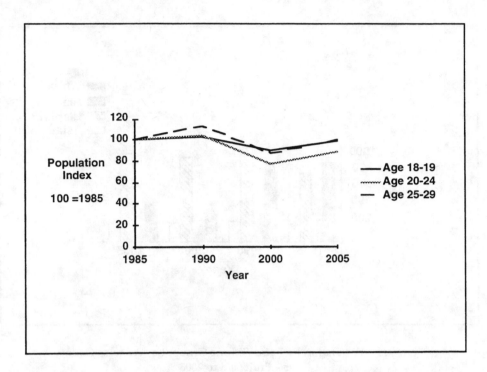

Figure 12—Projected Changes in Population of Those 18–29 Years Old in Los Angeles County

Source: California Department of Finance, Demographic Research Unit, *Population Projection*, March 1995.

The Ethnic Mix

The ethnic mix is also changing in the Los Angeles area, much more dramatically than that of the state as a whole. While there is evidence of steadily increasing minority participation state- and nationwide, as well as at CSUN, the rate at which minority participation increases will depend, among other things, on financial aid and affirmative action policies in the state. Because it is not possible to predict changes in these participation rates, our analysis is based on current knowledge about minority participation.

Figures 13 and 14 show population changes for four groups (white, black, Hispanic, and Asian/Other) in 1985 and 1990, along with projections for 2000 and 2005. Both white and black populations have declined, while the Hispanic population grew substantially from 1985 to 1990. Hispanics will continue to represent the largest group into the next century. The Asian/Other population remains stable.

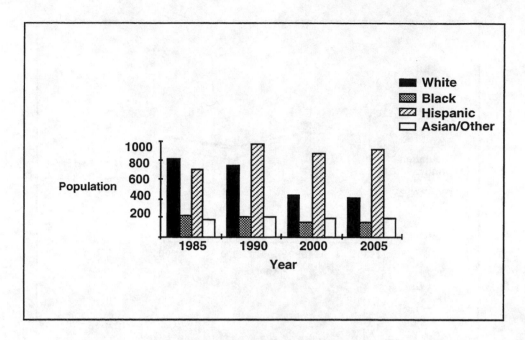

**Figure 13—Population by Racial/Ethnic Group, Los Angeles County
1985, Projected to 2005**

Source: California Department of Finance, Demographic Research Unit, *Population Projection*,
March 1995.

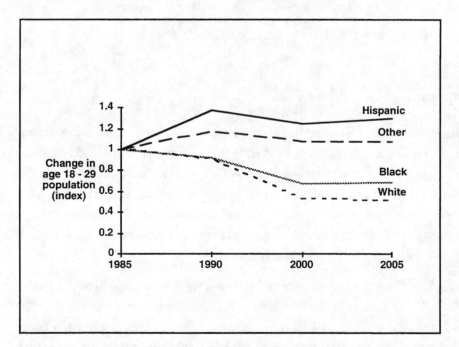

**Figure 14—Population Changes in Los Angeles and Ventura Counties Differ
by Racial/Ethnic Group**

Source: California Department of Finance, Demographic Research Unit, *Population Projection*,
March 1995.

These shifts have potentially important implications for CSUN enrollment demands because traditional participation rates in California and nationwide vary by race/ethnicity.   Figure 15 shows that the Hispanic population, which represents an increasingly large proportion of the population into the next century, did not enroll in CSUN at the same rates that other ethnic groups did from 1980 to 1994. This is consistent with college participation rates for Hispanics in general, which lag behind participation rates of whites, blacks, and Asians.

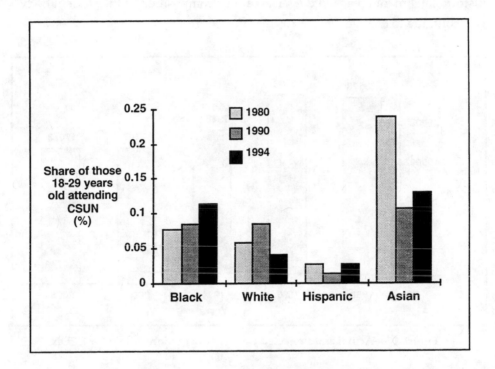

Figure 15—CSUN Undergraduate Participation Rates by Race/Ethnicity
(Percent of 18-29 Years Old Population within CSUN Catchment Area Attending CSUN
in Selected Years, by Race/Ethnic Group.)

Source: National Science Foundation CASPAR Database, 1994; CSUN Office of Institutional Research, Fall 1994.

Enrollment Projections[15]

Applying these county age and ethnic trends to the catchment area, and assuming that participation rates in the near future approximate current rates, projections indicate no return of CSUN enrollment and FTEs to 1980 and 1990 levels, and a shrinkage from 1994 levels (Figure 16). In sum, if current trends continue, aggregate enrollment will not return to pre-earthquake levels and will in fact decrease, fewer traditional-age students of any race or group will be in the historic catchment area, and the racial/ethnic composition of the student body will continue to change.

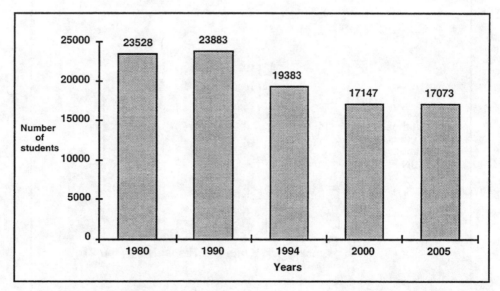

Figure 16—Actual and Projected Undergraduate Enrollment for CSUN

The enrollment decline represents an important difference between CSUN and the overall CSU system. For the system as a whole, projections indicate that enrollment demand will greatly outdistance the system's capacity to provide adequate facilities and services.[16] The enrollment decline seems quite surprising in view of enrollment demand projections that have been made by the University of California and other analysts, including RAND's own analysis, which predicts

---

[15]The actual population from which CSUN primarily draws enrollment is not all youth, but those who have attained eligibility for admission to CSU. The demographics of this "eligibility pool" do not necessarily correspond to the demographics of the larger population. For example, it is possible for the eligibility pool within the catchment area to expand, even if the local population is decreasing. Because there appear to be no clear trends with respect to eligibility pools in CSUN's catchment area, participation rates were assumed to be constant for purposes of this analysis. For further details of the demographic analysis, see the Technical Notes at the end of this report.

[16]Michael Shires, *The Future of Public Undergraduate Education in California*, Santa Monica, Calif.: RAND, MR-561-LE, 1996.

significant access deficits arising by 2010 in both the UC and CSU systems.[17] Shires projects continued increases in enrollment system-wide from 1995 to 2010, resulting in part from population increases beginning in 2005. The present analysis extends only to 2005.

However, the CSU enrollment demand differs so greatly from our estimate of CSUN enrollment levels because Los Angeles County trends (largely reflected in CSUN's catchment area) differ so significantly from overall state trends.

For example, between 1990 and 2000, the number of 20- to 24-year-olds drops by 219,612 in Los Angeles and Ventura Counties combined, and by 223,876 in the state as a whole. In other words, 98 percent of the projected decrease in this age group occurs in just two counties. Thus, this overall state trend can be expected to affect CSUN much more dramatically than it does many of the CSU campuses elsewhere in the state.

Among the 25- to 29-year-old population, California is projected to lose 476,770 total, with half that loss, 213,420 people, occurring in Los Angeles and Ventura Counties combined. Furthermore, while California's population should begin rising rapidly after 2000, Los Angeles and Ventura Counties will only begin to regain what they have lost. Los Angeles County population trends differ dramatically from aggregate state trends, as do Ventura County population trends (but to a lesser degree).

First-Time Freshmen Versus Transfer Enrollments

The preceding analysis focused on total undergraduate enrollments, but there are also implications for first-time freshman enrollment levels. As Figure 17 indicates, enrollments for first-time freshmen account for virtually all of CSUN's enrollment decline from 1990 to 1993, as compared with transfer enrollments, which remain stable. Over the last three years, it looks as if CSUN has not maintained its attractiveness for first-time freshmen. While our analysis does not identify the reasons for this brief trend, it may be linked to rising tuition levels. Despite tuition increases, CSU tuition remains well below other four-year colleges, both public and private, in its market area, as Figure 18 shows. However, the data we examined support the likelihood that more students may be opting to begin their college education at community colleges. Continued tuition increases at CSU could make this shift larger, implying that total

---

[17]Shires, Michael, ibid.

enrollment at CSUN (and other CSU campuses) will be lower and class distributions could become more heavily weighted toward upper-level students.

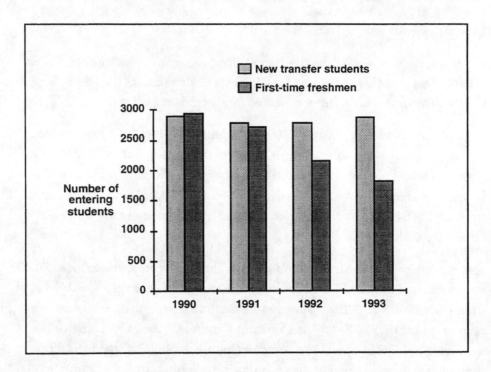

**Figure 17—Enrollments for First-Time Freshmen Account
for All of CSUN Drop**

Source: CSUN Office of Institutional Research, Student ERSS Files for various years.

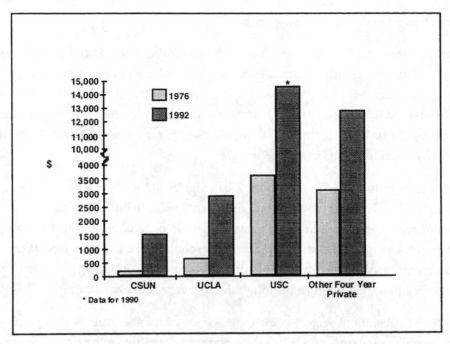

Figure 18—CSUN's Tuition Remains Competitive

Source: National Science Foundation CASPAR Database, 1994.

The Political Context

The information presented in the preceding sections is consistent with the findings of other analysts, with the perceptions of people in executive and legislative positions in Sacramento, and with the views of educational policy groups. These findings have serious implications, not only for the future of higher education but for the financial and social well-being of the state itself over the coming decades. While we have not attempted to systematically discuss our results among the political leadership in Sacramento, we have presented the results of these projections to politically diverse audiences in both northern and southern California, including those in the legislative and executive branches. We have also had numerous face-to-face interviews with political leaders and administrators and policymakers to discuss in detail the assumptions and conclusions contained in this report, as well as in RAND's reports on "three strikes" and on California's fiscal futures. In the following section we share some common responses to our analyses.

Constraints on Policy Response

Demographic trends imply continuing pressure for services, as the elderly and other receiver populations increase and as elementary and secondary school populations rise. Cuts in health and welfare support levels, which may continue, have enabled the state merely to maintain expenditure levels for these services. Our projections indicate that increasing demand for these services cannot be fully offset by continued cuts in service levels.

Policymakers and pundits see little hope of significant federal help with this situation: Block grants may increase program flexibility but will almost certainly mean further reductions in financial resources. In fact, federal budget action (proposed changes in Medicare, for instance) could make the state's position significantly worse. Finally, there is little of dramatic economic growth for California in the near future, although the recovery is likely to continue.[18]

While the substantial projected increase in corrections spending is recognized as a serious problem, the current public mood is not conducive to reforming the "three strikes" initiative. Unless law enforcement efforts and dollars can be redirected, the prison system will continue to absorb a rapidly growing share of California's fiscal resources.

The state already spends less per pupil on K–12 education than most other states. Thus, efforts to increase K–12 spending might seem more likely than efforts to cut it, even if that were advisable (or possible). Any increased expenditures on K–12 may come at the expense of higher education, creating a "zero-sum" scenario for educational interests in the state.

Within the postsecondary education community in California, the community colleges share the protection of Proposition 98. Thus, while their portion of revenues may not grow, it is unlikely to shrink and will therefore increase in proportion to funding available for CSU and the UC systems. Furthermore, many policymakers avowedly view the UC system as the "crown jewel" of the state's higher-education system, making it likely to get highest priority for support and financial restructuring or assistance. Both current retirement and salary policies threaten the quality of UC faculty and thus the UC system. CSU may thus anticipate that its needs will take second place to UC's.

---

[18]UCLA's widely watched quarterly report and economic forecast projects job growth of just 1.8 percent in California in 1995, compared with their earlier estimate of that for 3.5 percent. Job growth for 1996 is forecast at just 1.7 percent, 1997 at 2.8 percent.

Given all that, CSU and its individual campuses face a future of continued constraint and shrinkage of state financial resources, along with increasing demands for enrollment *for the system as a whole*. CSUN itself faces, at most, level demand for enrollment, combined with fiscal constraints and a changing demographic profile in its catchment area. If its enrollment demand shrinks, CSUN could lose resources through system reallocations to other campuses.

An Absence of Policy Guidance

State officials, elected office holders, and education policymakers to whom we have presented our research understand, and do not disagree, that the CSU system is highly vulnerable in this fiscal "crunch." However, in our discussions with them, no one outlined any plans for addressing the state's fiscal problems, or had specific guidance for how CSU should react to the scenario, or how it should adapt its mission or operations to ensure its survival. It was more often the case that those with whom we spoke were focused on short-term tactics to cope with emerging crises, rather than long-term strategies for the state's fiscal and educational futures.

It is important to remember that the comments and reactions described here do not flow from any sort of systematic opinion polling. They do represent, however, the prevailing outlook as we encountered it. Moreover, this outlook was consistent across party lines and throughout state government, and this consistency leads us to believe that including information about these reactions is an important component of this analysis. It indicates that CSUN in its planning effort cannot simply rely on state leadership to initiate timely and comprehensive responses to the fiscal scenario outlined herein. The current mindset in the state's political and policy community may reflect the shifting concerns of the state's voters, political uncertainties in Sacramento and Washington, D.C., and even the political effects of term limits in California.

One suggestion we heard with some frequency was that the CSU system needed to become more "productive." But there was little agreement as to how increased productivity could be achieved, beyond the conviction that greater use of "technology" would help.

A second suggestion was for CSU to reduce research and service activities, focusing more intensively on classroom teaching. The research mission of public higher education is being rethought in general—even though externally funded research brings in significant outside funding rather than simply imposing extra costs for many institutions and departments.

A third suggestion is to shift responsibility for remedial courses to community colleges and high schools, leaving the CSU system free to emphasize college-level work.

Beyond such general suggestions, there is no political consensus or even much speculation about the future of CSU or any of its individual campuses.

3. Conclusions and Implications for CSUN

Our projections suggest that California faces an unsettling fiscal future and that CSUN, along with the rest of the state's higher education system, will feel the effects. Besides fiscal constraints, CSUN must also contend with decreasing demand for enrollment, particularly for entering freshmen.

We cannot really predict what effect changes in the labor market will have on enrollment demand. However, if we could assume that local employment opportunities affect the decision to attend college, CSUN might expect a drop in demand: Our projections suggest that a high proportion of the jobs available in its catchment area will not require a college degree. The areas in which degree-requiring jobs are likely to be available might also affect the demand for certain programs at CSUN.

As we noted earlier, the environmental analysis is by no means exhaustive. Along the way, we have alluded to other issues that may be significant for CSUN's planners, including the following:

- CSUN's competitive position vis-a-vis other local four-year educational institutions, job training programs and community colleges, and other CSU campuses.

- How the level of educational preparation and language skills of incoming students might change and the implications for CSUN's program.

- How recent legislative developments and legal challenges (such as Proposition 187 and the affirmative-action debate, respectively) will affect the enrollment of immigrants and minorities.

These are just a few of the other environmental factors that raise complex educational challenges for CSUN.

What are the implications for CSUN's planning efforts? Most of our findings point clearly to one implication: CSUN cannot expect to operate as it has in the past—to continue with "business as usual." As the discussion of the political context implies, the fiscal problems are likely to get worse. Optimistically, our projections suggest that total support from the state will decline in real terms; pessimistically, that decline could be substantial. Nothing in the foreseeable future portends a fiscal turnaround. Moreover, our discussions with political leaders and education groups offered little hope of state action that would substantially change the scenario. In the likely fiscal and political context, pressures will be high for all the state's higher-education institutions to do more with less.

While the environmental picture is relatively clear, the conceptual and substantive implications for institutional-level policy changes are not. Conceptually, CSUN could accept the shrinking support and enrollments as inevitable and make plans for a minimalist kind of future—one in which it balances less support with smaller demand and develops a specialized mission in the larger CSU scheme of things. Alternatively, the strategic planning committee and the CSUN community at large might develop a strategy based on rethinking its goals and functions and establishing new or refocused priorities, and that addresses the support and enrollment challenges accordingly.

The Paradox of Planning

There is an inherent "paradox" in the presentation of the foregoing analysis to the CSUN community and to individuals engaged in the planning process. By its nature, this report focuses on factors that are outside CSUN's ability to control, such as California's fiscal situation, and macro-level demographic trends. Even if one takes issue with some of the specific assumptions underlying this report, its conclusions are robust. Thus the results of this analysis can be "paralyzing" in their effect on the planning process if planners do not perceive and trust in their ability to design and implement meaningful responses for the institution in this unfolding environment.

University leadership, and those who guide the planning effort, have the difficult task of framing the planning process in a way that avoids paralysis. As is documented in the literature on strategic planning and organizational change, if the community does not believe real change is possible, or if individuals feel threatened by the planning process itself, or if there is an undercurrent of mistrust or a lack of communication, planning can be thwarted. If participants do not believe the planning process is truly open or inclusive, the magnitude of the external challenges facing the university may be a convenient excuse for giving up on strategic planning.

In the course of our research it has become clear that CSUN has many strengths. It has several "signature" programs, for which it has become well-known nationwide. Many departments place a strong emphasis on undergraduate research, providing opportunities for effective marketing. The university has experienced recent successes in attracting and retaining Hispanic students, which can increase the proportion of that growing population that chooses CSUN over its competitors. There is a clear recognition within the university community of CSUN's opportunity to foster a diverse community and to provide leadership in the region and the state on dealing with issues of difference and diversity. These are just a few of the positive internal factors that are highly relevant to the responses CSUN may design to its external challenges.

One way to link the analysis contained in this report with university planning decisions is through the use of an internal information database to help identify options and opportunities for restructuring university programs, departments, and other units, as well as their related costs. As part of its technical assistance, RAND has supplemented CSUN's excellent internal research capabilities with such a comparative internal data system.

Substantively, campus decisionmakers may choose among numerous strategies in response to the projected trends. The environmental analysis is intended to help them by establishing common assumptions to guide the process. However, in the final analysis, only those involved in CSUN's strategic planning process can develop the strategies and make the choices based on this information and other inputs to the planning process.

Technical Notes: Demographic And Enrollment Projections

Readers desiring more detailed information about sources and methodology used in the analysis of California fiscal issues are referred to *Projecting California's Fiscal Future*, RAND, MR-570-LE, 1995. Details of demographic analysis presented in this report follow.

The projections contained in this report are intended to isolate and illustrate the potential effects of demographic changes in CSUN's prime catchment areas on future demand for CSUN's services. They are not intended to predict actual future enrollments. Given the lack of detailed pre-1990 data about CSUN's student population (because of destruction of data tapes during the Northridge earthquake), actual enrollment projections, which would require detailed longitudinal data to isolate and identify possible short- and long-term changes in enrollment behavior, could not be estimated. Nonetheless, the demographic composition of CSUN's traditional "catchment area" (defined below in section 2) has undergone and will continue to undergo dramatic changes, namely, declining numbers of traditional college-age individuals in the population and declines in sizes of ethnic groups that traditionally have had higher CSU participation rates. The authors felt it was important that the Strategic Planning Committee at CSUN be aware of the type and magnitude of these demographic changes and of their potential effects on enrollment.

In order to focus on the demographic impact, other factors that might affect CSUN enrollment rates were assumed to be constant. These factors include tuition rates and the availability of financial aid, trends in family incomes, labor market trends, changes in individual behavior, including the proportion of youngsters attaining eligibility in high school to attend CSU (i.e., completion of required courses), and CSUN's own efforts to increase applications, enrollment, and retention. Future enrollments at CSUN will, of course, depend on far more than the demographic situation; for example, potential declines in enrollment may be exacerbated by real increases in tuition or diminishing availability of financial aid; likewise, they may be mitigated by efforts at the secondary level to increase the numbers of minority (especially Hispanic) students who complete the college entrance requirements, and by CSUN's own outreach programs to high schools, which may influence student choice about whether and where to pursue a higher education degree. For information regarding the potential effects of these other factors in the near term, readers are referred to CSUN's Office of Institutional Research, *Enrollment Projections for 1995–96 to 1998–99*, April 10, 1995.

To assess the impact of demographic changes on enrollment it was necessary to (a) determine the geographic area from which CSUN has traditionally attracted the bulk of its students (its "prime catchment area"); (b) identify the age and ethnic composition of CSUN students over time; (c) compare CSUN's student population in terms of size, age, and race to its catchment area population over time, thereby determining participation rates by age and race; (d) estimate to the degree possible, based on population projections provided by the State of California, Department of Finance, the future demographic composition of CSUN's catchment area; and finally (e) use past participation rates by age and by race/ethnicity to estimate the numbers of students that CSUN might have, given projected changes in its catchment area population. In the following technical documentation, each of these steps will be briefly examined in terms of the types and limitations of the data sources used, assumptions that were made, and any further limitations of interpretation that may apply.

Research relied strongly on and is indebted to research conducted at CSUN itself, especially research produced by the Office of Institutional Research and the Geography and Business departments at CSUN. Special appreciation is due to Hans Ladanyi, Sujen-Sung, Dr. William Bowen, Javier Hidalgo, and Dean Taylor.

Determining the Catchment Area

As a starting point, we relied on the definition of CSUN's catchment area developed by a CSUN graduate business class, detailed in its report, "*The Mission of Cal State Northridge: Faculty Perceptions and Strategic Implications*," Brown et al., 1994. In this study, data on residential addresses were used to define a "core" CSUN catchment area encompassing northern Los Angeles County and eastern Ventura County (including Santa Clarita, Sylmar and San Fernando, parts of Glendale and Burbank, the east San Fernando Valley, and Malibu and West Los Angeles), and "fringe" areas (including areas in West Covina, Pomona, Hollywood, Inglewood, Whittier, Norwalk, Compton, Carson, South Pasadena, Arcadia, East Los Angeles, Long Beach, Manhattan Beach, and other cities in Ventura and Oxnard). Unfortunately, because of data limitations resulting from both the destruction of data in the Northridge earthquake and the type of data provided by CSUN, the definition of these catchment areas was based on analysis of students' addresses while attending CSUN, which would not necessarily reflect where students came from, but rather where they preferred to live while attending CSUN. RAND's research team faced similar data constraints, and, consequently, supplementary information on the county of students' permanent addresses, as well as data on the location of previous high school attended were used to adjust the boundaries of the prime catchment area. Actual permanent address data were not made available to RAND.

When determining the prime catchment area, RAND looked at high schools that had contributed larger numbers of students to CSUN. The population in the prime catchment area of those high schools was then added to CSUN's prime catchment area. The geographic area RAND identified as CSUN's prime catchment area encompassed entirely the "core catchment area" defined by the CSUN graduate school class, and included many of the fringe areas as well (for instance, Simi Valley, South Pasadena, Arcadia, Altadena, West Covina, Pomona and parts of East Los Angeles).

Data on the catchment area were analyzed by postal zip code areas. This approach has several implications, especially with regard to the definition of the prime catchment area for subsequent analysis. Not intended as geographic units of analysis, zip codes represent different- size geographic areas and populations that tend to change over time. Thus, "matching" the populations in the prime catchment area among the 1970, 1980, and 1990 census zip code data files (U.S. Bureau of the Census, STF3B) required considerable cleaning of data and making many assumptions. To help minimize the number of zip code boundaries that did not match among the census years, the core catchment area was ultimately defined as one large, geographically contiguous unit, thus limiting matching problems to the outer borders of the catchment area. This was done despite evidence that certain zip codes within the catchment area did not contribute many students to CSUN. The remaining "boundary" populations in those zip codes in the 1970 and 1980 censuses that crossed the outer boundaries of the catchment area as defined by 1990 zip code boundaries had to be reapportioned. Data available on alternative political and geographic units (on populations within city boundaries and census tract boundaries, for instance) were used to estimate the sizes and characteristics of boundary populations from the 1970 and 1980 censuses that needed to be excluded from the analysis. That is, based on analysis of other data sources regarding the geographic areas in question, we assumed that such populations would have been outside the prime catchment area if the 1970 and 1980 zip code boundaries coincided with the 1990 zip code boundaries.

It should be noted also that zip code boundaries can sometimes encompass large populations having quite diverse racial and socio-economic characteristics. CSUN may attract students from an area where one particular population is concentrated and not from other areas where other populations may predominate. This situation can also change over time. For this reason, the use of the less-detailed zip code boundaries can obscure some of the finer details of population characteristics. Nonetheless, analyses based on zip codes were deemed appropriate; without complete data on the permanent residence of students prior to entering CSUN, use of the additional detail that might have been provided by an analysis of census tract data would have been misleading: Such an analysis would have been based on census tract information about students' college-time residence, which in many cases would not represent the characteristics of the census tracts from which they originated.

Identifying the Age and Ethnic Composition of CSUN Population Over Time

For all years prior to and including 1992, data on age and ethnic composition of CSUN students were obtained from the National Science Foundation CASPAR database, October 1994, and cross-checked with the CSU Statistical Abstract. Post-1992 data were provided by CSUN's Office for Institutional Research. Racial and ethnic distributions are always based on percentages of identified students.

Identifying the Age and Racial/Ethnic Composition of CSUN's Prime Catchment Area Population

CSUN's catchment area population was analyzed using 1970, 1980, and 1990 U.S. Bureau of the Census STB3 data files (commonly referred to as "zip code files"). The catchment area population was matched among the years by the procedures defined above. As is well known, racial and ethnic categories changed considerably between censuses, and the 1970 census racial categorizations are not considered to be compatible with those of the 1980 and 1990 censuses. In 1970, for example, Asian-Americans were considered white and "Spanish-Americans" were considered a race. In 1980, the separation of race and Hispanic origin appeared, but these characteristics were not broken down by age group. Thus, for 1980 only, the population of those 18-29 years old is assumed to have the same race by Hispanic breakdown as the population as a whole. Consequently a small part of the increase in the proportion of Hispanics in the catchment area between 1980 and 1990 evidenced in the analysis may be attributable to this assumption. In fact, in-migrating Hispanics are generally younger individuals, and thus the proportion of Hispanics in 1980 may have been higher among those 18–29 years old than among the population as a whole. If that is the case, then this problem would contribute to an underestimation of the total Hispanic population in 1980. However, even if this is the case, the enrollment projections should not be affected significantly. Since enrollment projections were based on 1990 populations estimates, rather than 1980 estimates, published data for 1990 that included population figures broken down by race, age and Hispanic origin for Los Angeles County and Ventura County cities were used to identify the proportion of Hispanics in each racial/ethnic category.

Estimating Participation Rates over Time

There are three types of variation in higher-education participation behavior: short-term cyclical change—for example in response to fluctuations in labor markets, employment, or the demand for skills; longer-term behavioral changes attributable to changing perceptions of and attitudes toward the value of a higher degree itself or a particular institution granting degrees; and, finally, changes resulting from policy measures that affect supply or demand, such as the availability of financial aid and affirmative action policies. Behind these participation decisions are changing demographics that determine how many people are available to make such choices. Participation rates (the proportion of the relevant-age population that participates in higher education) vary from year to year, often considerably, and reflect the above short- and long-term changes in higher-education participation behavior as well as in demographics. In controlling for these changes and determining which participation rates would be projected into the future, this study was faced with a number of obstacles.

First, it was not possible to perform peak-to-peak analysis by race and age to determine the participation rates of CSUN's catchment population over time, which would have allowed us to carefully observe and control for short-term cyclical changes. Although county-level population estimates are available for every year, identifying the catchment population requires census data, which in this case limited the ability to derive such rates to just three points in time: 1970, 1980, and 1990. In addition, the above-mentioned problems with comparability of race data over time further limited our analysis to two years. To compensate for this lack, a rough peak-to-peak analysis was performed for the years 1980 to 1994 using county-level estimates of the group 18–29 years old by race (for Ventura and Los Angeles Counties) to ascertain whether 1990, the last year with available census and therefore catchment population data, might be an appropriate year upon which to base enrollment projections. This peak-to-peak analysis revealed that overall participation in 1990 was above average for the years studied, although 1990 was not the peak year. As a control, the catchment population, based on the 1990 census, was estimated to change at the same rates (stratified by age and race) as the populations of Ventura and Los Angeles Counties. Thus, a 1994 catchment population was estimated and comparison participation rates for 1994 (after the earthquake and after tuition increases) were derived.

CSUN has in recent years enrolled a stable number of students over 30 years of age (in 1993, 14.5 percent of student enrollment). The numbers of students 30 years of age and older was therefore assumed to remain constant. The enrollment projections include both the projected participation by those 18-29 years old, based on catchment population demographics and 1990 or 1994 participation rates by age and race for those 18-29 years old, and a constant number of individuals over 30 (which equaled the number of students 30 years and older who attended CSUN in 1993). The much larger older population (30-65 years old) would not be susceptible to the more dramatic demographic swings one might isolate within younger age groups. In addition, the participation of this group is so small compared with the catchment population as a whole that projections would be extremely sensitive.

Projections of the Catchment Area Population

Especially in Los Angeles, with its highly mobile population and high levels of immigration, population projections must be viewed with caution. The population projections used in this study were prepared by the California Department of Finance, Demographic Department, in March 1995. As no projections for the catchment population exist, it was broken down by county of origin and again by race and age.[19] Each group was then assumed to grow at the same rate as the corresponding group in the relevant county. As presented in the main text, comparisons of changes in county and catchment populations in 1970 to 1990 indicate that this assumption is reasonable.

Projections of the Effects of Demographic Changes on CSUN Enrollment

In a last step, the participation rates derived above (Section 4) for 1990 and 1994 were applied to the projected population of the catchment area as derived according to the method described in Section 5, above, and transformed into FTEs (assuming a 10.8-unit mean student load, 15 units equaling a course load).

---

[19]It should be noted that Department of Finance population projections identify only four racial/ethnic groups: white, black, Hispanic, and other, thus limiting the analysis performed in this research to these defined groups.

Although the projections based on the two years differed little from one another, the underlying dynamics of different racial and ethnic groups between the years were dramatic and worthy of discussion.

Though overall participation rates were higher in 1990 than in 1994, the participation rates of each racial and ethnic group changed markedly: in 1990, CSUN had only 2121 Hispanic undergraduates; by 1994 the number had more than doubled to 4593.[20] At the same time, the number of white undergraduates decreased enormously from 15,940 students in 1990 to 8,237 in 1994, a decline of close to 50 percent. It should be noted that despite these changes in participation, the numbers of first-time freshman Hispanics remained relatively stable. For example, 592 Hispanic first-time freshmen entered CSUN in the fall of 1990 (20 percent of all first-time freshmen). In 1991, this number increased to 594, and in 1992 the number dropped to 554 students. Thus, the overall increase in Hispanic students was largely the result of retention and increased numbers of Hispanic transfer students. At the same time, numbers and proportions of entering white and Asian first-time freshman students declined. White students represented 35.8 percent of entering freshmen (1057) and Asians 16.6 percent (490) in 1990, but the numbers dropped to 636 and 351 respectively, by 1992.

These unusually dramatic changes pose problems for the educational demographer as the participation rates for members of different racial and ethnic groups changed much more rapidly than their source populations did. Consequently, projections were done based on both 1990 and 1994 participation rates by race/ethnicity. It is precisely the dramatic changes in participation rates that explain the small numeric difference between the two enrollment projections. That is, the effect of the drop in participation by white students between 1990 and 1994 is offset by the increase in Hispanic participation rates, coupled with a large increase in Hispanic population, over the same period.

Another way to project enrollments might have been to use the eligible population, i.e. the number of students completing the entrance requirements, instead of using the entire age group.

There are problems with this approach. First, the rates at which high school graduates complete CSU entrance requirements among CSUN's feeder schools appear to be stable, so there is no evidence that increases will occur in these completion rates to offset the effects of the decline in the overall student population. Estimating the entire age-relevant population has the same effect as

---

[20]This number is so large as to seem unbelievable. These numbers were obtained and verified by Hans Ladanyi at CSUN's Office of Institutional Research, who confirmed that such a dramatic increase in Hispanic undergraduate students had indeed occurred.

holding high school completion rates constant, which thus seems to be a reasonable analytic strategy. Second, whereas completion rates, when multiplied by the age-relevant population, do provide projections of first-time enrollments, the problem of estimating future transfer enrollments would still remain. There are no clear trends in community college participation in Los Angeles and Ventura Counties on which to base estimates of any increases or decreases in these transfer enrollments.

Given these uncertain trajectories, projections in this report are based on the entire age-range population. This approach assumes that (a) numbers of students completing entrance requirements will remain constant over the relevant time horizon; (b) the numbers of these students who will chose to attend CSUN will remain constant; and (c) the number of community college transfer students will remain constant.

Finally, it is of interest to note that there is no firm evidence that the recent decline in CSUN attendance rates is attributable to the loss of students to other institutions in the Los Angeles County/Ventura County area.

Finally, it is of interest to note that there is no firm evidence that the recent decline in CSUN attendance rates is attributable to the loss of students to other institutions in the Los Angeles County/Ventura County area. Enrollment rates at other public four-year institutions have, on average, been fairly stable since 1984, and private four-year college enrollments have increased only slightly since the mid-1980s. Between 1990 and 1992, as CSU tuition rates were greatly increasing and enrollment rates at almost all Los Angeles County and Ventura County CSU campuses were declining, community college enrollment rates increased by 12 percent, suggesting that at least some eligible students were choosing to complete the first two years at a community college. In 1991, the Los Angeles and Ventura community colleges did experience a severe drop in enrollment. In 1993, the state substantially raised tuition at community colleges for degree-holders, and roughly 38 percent of the enrollments drop after 1992 can be accounted for by students who already possessed a bachelor's degree. These students would not have been candidates for undergraduate enrollment at CSUN. However, another 55.4 percent of the enrollment decline was accounted for by fewer first-time freshmen. This decline was likely a reflection of the economic recovery, which diverted some students into employment, as well as of decreased numbers of high school graduates in 1992.